Who Was That Dog I Saw You With, Charlie Brown?

Charles M. Schulz

CORONET BOOKS
Hodder Fawcett Ltd., London

First published by Fawcett Publications, Inc.,
New York, 1973
Coronet edition 1974
This book comprises the first half of
You're You, Charlie Brown, and is reprinted by
arrangement with Holt, Rinehart & Winston, Inc.

Copyright © 1967, 1968 by
United Feature Syndicate, Inc.

Printed and bound in Great Britain for
Coronet Books,
Hodder Fawcett Ltd,
St. Paul's House, Warwick Lane,
London, EC4P 4AH
by Hazell Watson & Viney Ltd,
Aylesbury, Bucks

ISBN 0 340 17861 2

→

→

HOW IN THE WORLD DO YOU FIND A SNOW-COVERED SUPPER DISH?!

Schulz

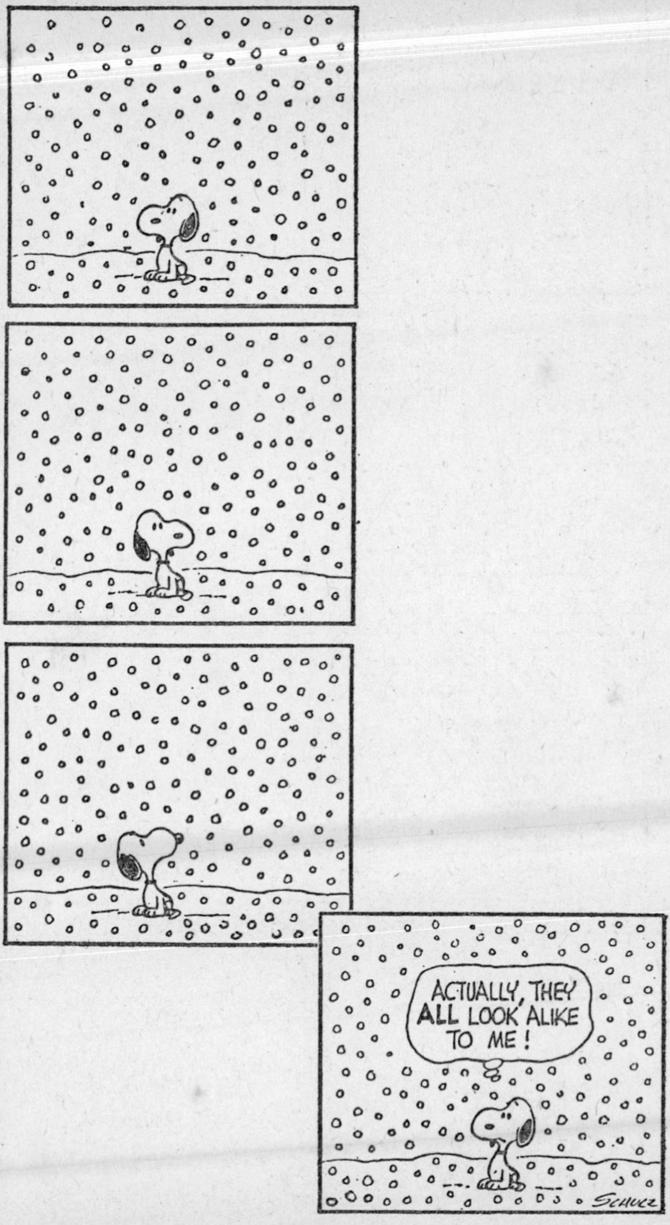
ACTUALLY, THEY ALL LOOK ALIKE TO ME!
SCHULZ

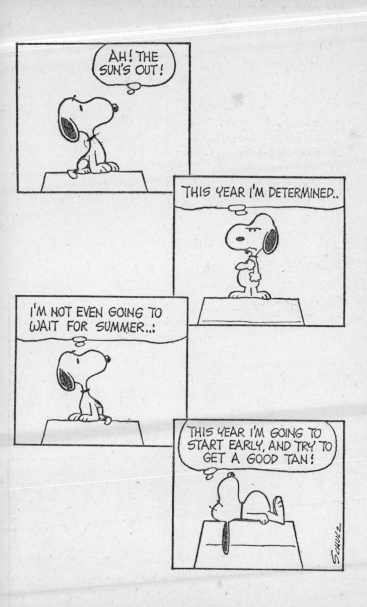

HAPPY FATHER'S
DAY from
your rare gem.

HI, ROY...I SUPPOSE
YOU'RE WONDERING
WHAT I'M DOING...

I'VE JUST MADE MY DAD A
HAND-MADE FATHER'S DAY CARD..

THIS IS THE SAME THING I HAD TO EAT YESTERDAY..
IN FACT, THIS IS THE SAME THING I HAD TO EAT EVERY DAY FOR THE PAST MONTH!
I THINK I'LL REGISTER A COMPLAINT...
AFTER I'VE FINISHED EATING!
SCHULZ

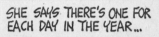

© 1970 United Feature Syndicate, Inc.

Wherever Paperbacks Are Sold

All these books are available at your bookshop or newsagent, or can be ordered direct from the publisher. Just tick the titles you want and fill in the form below

....

CORONET BOOKS, P.O. Box 11, Falmouth, Cornwall.

Please send cheque or postal order. No currency, and allow the following for postage and packing:

1 book – 7p per copy, 2–4 books – 5p per copy, 5–8 books – 4p per copy, 9–15 books – 2½p per copy, 16–30 books – 2p per copy in U.K., 7p per copy overseas.

Name ....

Address ....

....